WEDDING GUIDE

for the Best Man

JO PACKHAM

A STERLING/CHAPELLE BOOK
Sterling Publishing Co. Inc.   New York

Jo Packham, author
Dave Simon, co-author
Reva S. Petersen, designer

Library of Congress Cataloging-in-Publication Data

Packham, Jo.
  Wedding guide for the best man / by Jo Packham.
     p. cm.
  "A Sterling/Chapelle book."
  Includes index.
  ISBN 0-8069-0837-8
  1. Wedding etiquette.   I. Title.
BJ2065.B47P33   1994
395' .22--dc20
                                          94-12875
                                            CIP

10 9 8 7 6 5 4 3 2

A Sterling/Chapelle Book

Published by Sterling Publishing Company, Inc.
387 Park Avenue South, New York, NY 10016
©1994 by Chapelle Ltd.
Distributed in Canada by Sterling Publishing
c/o Canadian Manda Group, P.O. Box 920, Station U
Toronto, Ontario, Canada M8Z 5P9
Distributed in Great Britain and Europe by Cassell PLC
Villiers House, 41/47 Strand, London WC2N 5JE, England
Distributed in Australia by Capricorn Link (Australia) Pty Ltd.
P.O. Box 6651, Baulkham Hills, Business Center, NSW 2153, Australia
Manufactured in the United States of America
All Rights Reserved

Sterling ISBN 0-8069-0837-8

Contents

The Modern Best Man's Responsibilities: Showing Up!

The Traditional Best Man's Responsibilities: See the following—

Introduction

*A*sking someone to be a wedding partici-
pant, especially one as important as best man,
is not only an ancient custom but an honor and
a great responsibility. In the past, there were
definite rules about whom should be asked,
absolute guidelines on what his role should be,
and a well-defined area of responsibility.

Today, however, with modern mobility,
career obligations, and scattered families, the
decision of who is selected to be best man is
usually decided upon by the groom with the
help of his bride-to-be. The best choice for best
man is usually reached after the bride and
groom's, their families' and their other wedding
participants' needs and wants have been thor-
oughly discussed.

The choice for best man is usually made with great care so as not to hurt anyone's feelings, all the while satisfying the needs and wants of the groom and his fiancé.

The groom did not ask you to stand by his side because of a feeling of obligation. Such an important position should never be made based on family feelings or past obligations. Nor should he have asked you to be his best man just because he was your best man. Nor should he feel obligated for any other reason. The groom should never have to hear:

"So, you chose Hector — that two-faced ingrate — to be your best man. . . . HOW COULD YOU? After all we've been through!

"Consider our friendship **d-i-s-s-o-l-v-e-d!**"

Or he should never have to find an excuse such as:

"But . . . but, Joe . . . please try and understand. I would've picked you — you know I would have — but Amanda, the Psychic Wedding-Attendant-Astrologer-Coordinator advised my bride-to-be against it. Something about our moons clashing. She said the two of us standing side by side would be like hiring an annulment attorney to be the minister!"

The groom probably contacted you immediately after the engagement was announced. He did this at the same time his bride asked her maid/matron of honor to participate, and immediately before they both contacted the other wedding party participants.

The invitation to participate should have been issued in person or, if you live a great distance from the groom, by telephone or in a handwritten letter.

You should never refuse the honor of being best man unless it is absolutely impossible for you to do so. If you are forced to withdraw from the wedding party unexpectedly, an acceptable excuse would be a death in the family; a lame excuse would be the death of your goldfish.

If this does occur, the groom can ask one of the other groomsmen to take your place. This can be done even up to the day prior to the wedding. The groom can then leave the groomsman's position vacant or ask another family member or close friend to take this person's place. Friends or family members should not be offended by such a late invitation from the groom, but rather should be flattered that he feels close enough to count on them in an emergency.

Remember that not everyone that is asked to be a best man, even you, may be aware of all of his responsibilities — even if you have been a best man six or seven times you may have not done all you should have. You especially may not know exactly what to do if you are young or if you have never participated in a wedding before.

The groom should not assume that you know what is expected of you, and you should not hesitate to talk to him about his expectations and your duties. You may even wish to have his bride-to-be included in this discussion because she, too, will have definite ideas on your responsibilities and how she wants some of them to be executed.

The groom should never expect more of his best man than the individual can reasonably afford to give — both in time and financial considerations. He should want his wedding to be as memorable for those closest to him as he does for the bride and himself.

The Best Man's Responsibilities

Most Westerners — even tribesmen who have never been out of the jungle — know that the best man stands beside the groom during the wedding ceremony. What is less known is that he sits on the bride's RIGHT during the bridal dinner, unless, on account of his table  manners, she wishes him to sit bibbed and by himself at a separate table (possibly in the next room).

You and the groom will want to review all of the possibilities and then, with the bride-to-be, itemize your duties on a work sheet. You should then keep a copy for yourself, the bride should keep a copy, and the groom should keep a copy.

Historically, the best man was the groom's brother or his closest friend. Nowadays, time constraints being what they are, you could be a complete stranger. (The groom may have checked his friendly Yellow Pages under "FOR RENT: Wedding Attendants," to find your name.)

Seriously, in today's society, especially if this is his second marriage, the groom may choose his father, his grandfather, his son — or his brother or best friend to be his best man. Next to the groom and his bride, the best man shares with the maid/matron of honor the distinction of being the most important member of the wedding party. You are the one who will help the groom with some of the decision making, you are the one who will always be there to bolster the groom's confidence, and you are the one who will supply all of the necessary reassurance and support. Your duties are many and your responsibilities are important, for you will need to relieve the groom of as many details and as much responsibility as possible.

If there is no wedding coordinator, the best man, the maid/matron-of-honor, and the wedding hosts are responsible for making certain that the ceremony and reception go exactly as planned. You are the one who should be prepared for and handle any emergency!

You, therefore, should be the friend or relative that was selected over any other, not only because you are the closest to the groom, but because you are the most responsible and dependable (unless you have the confidence and emotional stability of a two-year-old) and, in his opinion, have the best sense of humor!

He should not hear you say:

"I don't know if I can give a toast in front of 500 people. You know how nervous I get. I'm palpitating just thinking about it! Look—my hands!"

Nor should he have to reassure you by saying: "Would you RELAX? It is only going to be the immediate families!"

The traditional best man's responsibilities:

1. You, as the best man, will assist the groom with any necessary arrangements. This includes ensuring he arrives at his wedding, clothed and conscious;

or counseling, coordinating and arranging any last-minute changes in plans.

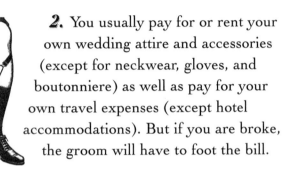

2. You usually pay for or rent your own wedding attire and accessories (except for neckwear, gloves, and boutonniere) as well as pay for your own travel expenses (except hotel accommodations). But if you are broke, the groom will have to foot the bill.

3. You take charge of the groomsmen the groom has selected and make certain they each know their responsibilities. You, also, work very closely with the head usher selected by the groom and give to him some of the responsibility for the groomsmen.

4. You, as the best man, are required to attend all pre-wedding festivities that you are invited to, including the rehearsal and rehearsal dinner. You should be aware that substitutions are generally frowned upon by the groom and his bride-to-be and that you are generally expected to make clever, appropriate conversation throughout, i.e., "I ate a worm once!"

5. Some time before the wedding, either with the ushers or with their approval, you should select the gift that you and the grooms-men will present to the groom. You are responsible for all details of the gift: collecting the money, making certain it is engraved or printed, and presenting it to the groom on everyone's behalf (usually at the rehearsal dinner or the bachelor party/dinner).

You might consider something such as an engraved wedding plaque that says:

> *To Marvin, You lucky devil,*
> *You handsome newt,*
> *To be married to Myra,*
> *What a hoot. . . .*
> *From the Wedding Gang*

You are also required to give a gift of your own to the wedding couple.

6. You make certain the groom's formal attire is picked up before the wedding, ideally with enough time for him to put it on before the ceremony begins.

7. You help the groom pack for his honeymoon and double-check all of the details: money or travelers' checks, passports, car keys, transportation, tickets, hotel reservations, prescription drugs, insect repellent and so on.

You also make certain the clothes the groom will wear when he leaves the reception are packed in a different bag than the clothing for his honeymoon. You then mark both bags and deliver them to the reception site, unless you are totally clueless about the right or wrong way to pack a suitcase, in which case you will leave everything to the groom.

8. You organize and host the bachelor party or dinner, unless it is just you and the groom, in which case you might choose to lecture him unrelentingly about marital affairs, the birds and the bees, contraceptives, the perpetual and unrelenting sacrifices and compromises required of a happy, enduring marriage, and on and on until he may wish he had asked someone else to be his best man.

9. You help the bride's mother with any last-minute arrangements or chores for the wedding or the reception.

10. You make certain the groom is dressed in plenty of time and has the marriage license in his pocket, and you drive the groom to the wedding ceremony. That is, unless you are running late, in which case the groom may opt to drive — often at speeds approaching the sound barrier — to ensure his bride does not elope with one of the ushers to save face.

Of course, the best man cannot expect to have COMPLETE CONTROL over the groom; no, life rarely offers such luxuries, unless you are a licensed voodoo doctor.

Generally speaking, however, in most North American weddings, the best man will NOT be a witch doctor. A quack, possibly; a necromancer, no.

So the best man — usually someone with no leadership or trance-inducing skills whatsoever (except in the mind of the groom), simply prods the groom along as best he can. In all but rare occasions, this is usually sufficient to get the job done.

11. The best man makes certain that the ushers are on time, properly dressed, and briefed again about the ceremony procedures and their responsibilities.

If the groom makes these chores of yours a physical impossibility, you may find it necessary to call one of the ushers for help and explain:

"Hello, John, it's Dave, the best man. Listen, we're running a little late. Are you dressed?

"WHAT!? . . . . . . YOU'RE IN THE SHOWER?!?"

12. You hold the ring to be given to the bride until it is time to exchange rings during the ceremony, unless the ring bearer is doing so. If a rehearsal is held, it should be made clear at that time not only WHO will hold the ring but WHEN the officiant will ask for it.

NOTE: To execute a smooth and timely ring exchange, you must make certain that the reverend or rabbi gives the SAME SPEECH he gave at the rehearsal, not ad-lib entire sections, as was the case in the wedding of a friend of mine.

He tells of the reverend going on and on about the bride's life-to-be — a Cinderella-like one of submission, compliance, and obedience, when suddenly the reverend paused and looked at the groom, who turned and looked at Dave, the best man.

The groom whispered, "The ring, dummy."

Dave said, "Oh," and began looking in vain for the ring, which was caught in the hem of the pocket of his tux pants.

A HINT FOR THE BEST MAN: *NEVER* put the ring in your trouser pocket, where it could remain indefinitely. Keep it, instead, in your vest pocket or lodged tightly between your thumb and index finger, like a hydraulic press, so when the officiant surprises you, you will be ready!

13. The best man enters the church or temple immediately after the groom and stands next to him during the ceremony.

The best man should exhibit his best behavior; giving the groom wet-willies, whispering during the ceremony, or taking bathroom breaks reflects somewhat juvenile behavior.

14. You escort the maid/matron-of-honor down the aisle during the recessional, taking special care not to (a) upstage the newlyweds, or (b) become entangled in the bride's dress.

15. The best man is in charge of and signs the marriage certificate as a witness if he is 18 years or older (which is the required age for signing a legal document). If you are not old enough, have extremely illegible handwriting, or cannot keep your signature from roaming all over the certificate, rendering it unreadable, the groom's father or an older usher can sign the certificate for you.

16. You make certain to get all payment checks from the groom or his father and then give one payment check to the officiant either just before or immediately after the ceremony.

You may also disperse similar checks to service providers as needed, possibly noting the amounts in a ledger or on a computer spreadsheet for tax purposes.

(Certainly, some of these checks may have to be obtained from members of the bride's family if they think they can trust you.)

17. Immediately following the recessional or receiving line, you see both the groom and the bride to the waiting car. In the absence of a chauffeur, you are the one who drives the two of them to the reception.

If the car has been stolen, you may be required to carry the two of them ON YOUR

BACK, camel-style. You should carry gloves so that you will be prepared, just in case.

If there is a chauffeur, you will usually drive the maid/matron of honor and the bridesmaids who do not have transportation to the reception.

18. Along with the official wedding hosts, you attend to any emergencies that might arise during the ceremony or reception.

19. You help gather the groomsmen together for all formal picture taking before and after the ceremony and during the reception. A truly thoughtful best man — one with the photographer's sanity in mind — does this by actually binding the groomsmen together with a long, sturdy rope.

20. If the bride chooses to have you do so, you stand in the receiving line. If you have been bad — for example, you fell asleep during the ceremony — she may make you stand in the corner with your nose to the wall.

Otherwise, you mingle with the guests and see to your other responsibilities. If there is a bridal dinner, you sit on the bride's right.

21. It is your responsibility to make the first toast to the groom and his bride and to announce or introduce family members. You will also read any telegrams or messages that have arrived.

(You should keep the telegrams for safe-keeping and deliver them to the bride's parents immediately after the reception or to the bride on her return from her honeymoon.)

Naturally, toasts vary in length. A good rule of thumb is to keep them between three and four seconds long. Anything shorter and the guests will feel cheated and confused. (See page 44 for possibilities.)

22. You are the first to dance with the bride after the groom, his father-in-law, and his father.

You then dance with both mothers, the maid/matron-of-honor, and other female attendants. In short, you should feel obligated to dance with every woman at the wedding — every young man's dream come true!

23. Immediately before the groom and his bride choose to leave the reception, you are responsible for escorting both families to the dressing rooms for their farewells. You will then lead the groom and the bride through the waiting guests to the door.

24. You are in charge of the transportation that will be used to leave the reception, and you keep these plans secret and the car hidden so as to avoid any practical jokes. (At one wedding, the plans were so secret that the best man didn't even know about them.)

You make certain that the groom and bride's luggage is in the car. Then, you are personally responsible for driving the two of them to a hidden automobile or for making the arrangements to have the car delivered immediately before their departure.

25. You arrange to have flowers or a bottle of chilled champagne (or warm milk if you feel it is more appropriate) delivered to the couple's hotel room just before their arrival.

As tempting as it may sound, hiding in the new couple's honeymoon suite closet and waking them up in the middle of the night dressed as Edward Scissorhands is a no-no.

26. You make certain to return the groom's wedding attire (if it was rented) or keep his personally owned attire until he returns from the honeymoon. Hocking the groom's personally owned tux is a good way of testing the staying power of your friendship.

27. You organize the return of all groomsmen's rented formal wear, or delegate the responsibility to another groomsman:

"Take care of everything, would you, Dave?"

You also deposit money gifts into appropriate accounts, and work with the honor attendant to make certain all wedding gifts are delivered to a predetermined location.

Coordinating the Groomsmen/Ushers

*T*raditionally, a groomsman was selected by the groom as an escort for a bridesmaid and an usher was at the wedding strictly to seat guests before the ceremony. And the rule of thumb was to have one usher for every fifty guests, assuming that one-half to three-fourths of the invited guests would attend.

In today's society, however, the roles are combined, the terms are used interchangeably and there may be any number of groomsmen and/or ushers the groom and bride decide upon.

You, as best man, will need to know whether or not the groom has chosen one groomsman for each of the bridesmaids and then asked additional individuals to be ushers, or whether he selected the option of having all groomsmen serve as ushers, seating guests before the ceremony and joining the wedding party shortly before the ceremony.

Be certain to inquire as to whether he is having all of his groomsmen usher and then join the wedding party or whether he has elected to have one or more remain behind to seat the late arrivals.

You will need to know which usher was selected as the head usher and whether he wishes for you to assign junior users the same duties as older ushers, which could include walking in the processional and recessional, or whether the groom chooses for the junior usher simply to stand near the entrance to the ceremony site to seat the late arrivals.

You will, also, need to know which of the groomsmen are family and which are friends.

Also, find out if there are any special circumstances or uneasy feelings between members of the wedding party, so that you can take actions to avoid problems.

You will need to get a list from the groom, or meet with him and make a list, of who the groomsmen are and what their responsibilities will be so that you can divide them among the groomsmen and make certain each responsibility is carried out.

It is important that as the best man you come to know all of the groomsmen. Do not be afraid to ask the groom details about each one that will help you to know them better and quicker.

To help you, the groom may tell you such things as:

"Tiffany, the matron-of-honor, used to date Bob, the head usher, until she caught him with Kasha, the second matron-of-honor.

"At the time, Kasha was dating Sam, the second groomsman-in-command and a close friend of Bob's. . . . Sam and Bob haven't spoken since. I was hoping the wedding would break the ice. . . .

"Tiffany and Sam then began dating until he caught her with Melanie, the third maid-of-honor.

"Did I mention that Bob and Melanie are slightly delusional and have been known to carry small concealed weapons?

"Not that I think there will be any trouble. I just thought you might like to know."

As you continue reading you will find most responsibilities for the groomsmen in the list that follows; you and the groom, however, may wish to add a few of your own.

A. The usher that has been selected to be the head usher will work closely with you, the best man. He will help supervise the other ushers and be responsible for any tasks you or the groom assign to him.

You then assign the other ushers certain aisles at the ceremony site. You will often hear such things as:

"I want to seat the late arrivals."

"No, I do."

"No, me."

"I do, I do; please pick me."

"I've got the nicest tux, so I get to."

Based on this important input and data, you must make your decisions.

You, also, should make certain that the head usher is in charge of special seating arrangements, and that he has a pew seating chart available in case of questions or forgotten pew cards. It is also the head usher who identifies special guests, such as a favorite aunt, and sees they are seated toward the front.

The head usher usually takes the responsibility of seeing that all of the other ushers arrive at the wedding site on time for both the rehearsal and the ceremony.

B. You make certain all of the groomsmen understand they are usually responsible to pick up, pay for, or rent their own wedding attire and all accessories (except their gloves, neckwear and boutonnieres, which are given to them by the groom).

They also pay for their own travel expenses (except for hotel accommodations, which should be paid by the groom unless other arrangements are made).

C. You inform them of the appropriate protocol of attending all pre-wedding parties to which they are invited and the rehearsal and rehearsal dinner, and that they may, singly or jointly with you, the best man, host the bachelor's party or other pre-wedding parties.

D. You make certain all groomsmen contribute to a joint gift to the groom, which is traditionally selected and presented by you, the best man.

E. Make certain they understand they should arrive at the wedding site approximately one hour before the ceremony begins.

F. You direct the groomsmen to seat arriving guests before the ceremony, asking if they are friends or relatives of the bride or groom. They should also make polite but quiet conversation with the guests as they escort them to their seats.

Instruct them to offer their right arm to each woman while her escort follows behind.

If several women arrive together, the eldest should be seated first. An elderly man alone can also be accompanied to his seat by an usher. In traditional Christian services, the bride's guests are on the left, the groom's on the right (the opposite is true in Jewish services).

If one section has many more guests than the other, you see that the usher seats the guests on the side with more available seats. (For more detailed information on ceremony seating, see *Wedding Ceremonies* by Jo Packham, page 75.)

G. If one of the ushers is a brother of the groom or the bride, you remind him that he is the one who will escort his own mother to her proper place. If not, he will seat the bride's mother in the left front pew and the groom's parents in the right front pew.

He must also be made aware that the groom's parents are to be seated five minutes before the bride's mother. When her mother is seated, it is a signal that the processional is about to begin and no other guests are to be seated after that time.

If either the bride's or the groom's parents are divorced, the bride's mother and her husband should be seated in the first pew. Her father and his wife are seated in the second pew (unless the groom and the bride have decided it is appropriate to have both parents and spouses sit together in the first pew).

H. Make certain one or several of the groomsmen perform other pre-ceremony functions such as distributing programs, rolling out an aisle runner, lighting candles, or setting up pew ribbons.

I. Coach the groomsmen to precede or escort, whichever style the bride has selected, the bridesmaids down the aisle during the processional and escort the bridesmaids during the recessional.

J. Choose one or several of the ushers to return to the front of the church or temple after the recessional to loosen the pew ribbons; escort the bride's mother and the groom's mother, honored elderly, or disabled guests out of the building first; and then return and signal the other guests to file out, row by row, from front to back.

K. Appoint an usher to make certain that all belongings of the wedding party and guests have been cleared before leaving the ceremony site.

L. Select one or more ushers to give directions to the reception site and make certain that all guests have transportation.

M. See that the ushers transport the bridesmaids and out-of-town guests throughout the wedding day, if necessary.

N. Lead the ushers so that they sit at the bridal table alternating with the bridesmaids.

O. Make certain they know that unless instructed otherwise by the bride, the groomsmen do not stand in the receiving line but mingle with the guests and dance with the bridesmaids and other single female guests.

They also participate in all reception activities and should encourage all single male guests to participate in the garter ceremony.

P. Reiterate that it is the ushers' responsibility to help in any capacity whenever needed during both the ceremony and the reception.

Q. Remind them that all ushers need to stay available for formal pictures before or after the ceremony and during the reception.

R. Make certain that all ushers help other wedding party members with post-reception duties such as making sure all gifts are transferred to a secure location, making certain that all of the flowers are delivered, and checking that nothing is left behind at the reception site.

Wedding Toasts for the Best Man

*T*he custom of drinking a "toast" to the prosperity, happiness, luck, or good health of another dates back to antiquity.

It is impossible to point to the moment when the first crude vessel was raised in honor of an ancient god, but what we do know is that the custom of drinking to health permeated the ancient world and that over time the simple act of toasting another became embellished and intertwined with other customs.

At some point along the way, toasts were created to celebrate success, happiness, and all other emotions or events worth honoring. Some time after the Seventeenth Century, the

gesture of clinking glasses became popular.
One legendary explanation for such glass
clinking is that all five senses should come into
play to get the greatest pleasure from a drink.
It is tasted, touched, seen, smelled, and — with
the clink — heard.

The popularity of toasting today is evident
with the many events and established protocols
of who should toast whom and when. On
many occasions, toasting may go on for several
hours so that everyone has an opportunity to
offer their good wishes.

From the time the groom and his bride-to-be
become engaged until the end of their wedding
day, there will be several "dictated" as well as
spontaneous occasions on which you as the
best man will want to deliver a toast or speech.
The dictated occasions are as follows:

Rehearsal Dinner: First is the customary
salute to the couple by the best man. The

groom then follows with a toast to his bride and his new in-laws; then the bride toasts the groom and his family. Others may follow.

Reception: The wedding toast is traditionally given by the best man. You should talk of how the groom and the bride met and a few words about the hopes the two of them have for their future.

At the end of the toast you raise your glass and toast to the bride and groom, and all guests raise their glasses and join in the toast.

The bride then places her arm through the groom's and they both drink. The locking arms signify the intertwining of their new lives. The groom may then respond by thanking you, the best man, and toasting the bride, his new in-laws and his parents.

The bride then adds her own toast honoring the groom and his family and thanking her parents.

Several ideas for toasts that you can use are listed below. For a more comprehensive list, see *Wedding Toasts and Speeches, Finding the Perfect Words*, by Jo Packham.

Traditional Toasts

A health to you,
A wealth to you,
And the best that life can give to you.
May fortune still be kind to you.
And happiness be true to you,
And life be long and good to you,
Is the toast of all your friends to you. ❤

Nothing is worth more than this day. ❤
—Goethe

Coming together is a beginning;
keeping together is progress;
working together is success. ❤ —Henry Ford

May the two of you breakfast with Health,
dine with Friendship, crack a bottle with Mirth,
and sup with the goddess of Contentment. ❤

Always remember to forget the trouble that passes
away, but never forget to remember the blessings that
come each day. ❤

To every lovely lady bright,
I wish a gallant faithful knight;
To every faithful lover, too,
I wish a trusting lady true. ❤
—Sir Walter Scott

Down the hatch, to a striking match! ❤

May the special moments of today be the most remembered memories of tomorrow. ❤

With trumpets and fanfare,
I wish you the happiest of all days. ❤

May your eyes stay filled with stars and your hearts with visions of dreams yet to come. ❤

May you always share your love and laughter. ❤

May you have enough happiness to keep you sweet; enough trials to keep you strong; enough sorrow to keep you human; enough hope to keep you happy; enough failure to keep you humble; enough success to keep you eager; enough friends to give you comfort; enough faith and courage in yourselves to banish depression; enough wealth to meet your needs; and enough determination to make each day a better day than yesterday. ❤

The man or woman you really love will never grow old to you. Through the wrinkles of time, through the bowed frame of years, you will always see the dear face and feel the warm heart union of your eternal love. ❤
—Alfred A. Montapert

For lovers who keep on keeping on with their love, there is never an end to the glories of marriage. ❤

People spend their lives in anticipation of being extremely happy in the future. But all you own is the PRESENT . . . NOW. PAST opportunities may, or may not, come. NOW is all you have. You must enjoy each day—one at a time. You are here on a short visit. Be sure to smell the flowers. ❤   —Alfred A. Montapert

I wish you the time to celebrate the simple joys. ❤

The way to Happiness: Keep your heart free from hate, your mind from worry. Live simply. Expect little. Give much. ❤

A program for happiness—
To live content with small means;
To seek elegance rather than luxury,
and refinement rather than fashion;
To be worthy, not respectable;
and wealthy, not rich;
To study hard, think quietly,
talk gently, act frankly;
To listen to the stars and birds;
to babes and sages with open hearts;
To bear all cheerfully, and bravely,
await occasions, hurry never;
In a word, to let the spiritual, unbidden and uncon-
scious, grow up through the common. ❤
—William Henry Chandler

When love is concerned;
too much is not ever enough. ❤
—Pierre-Augustin Caron de Beaumarchais

Love is what you go through together. ❤
—Thornton Wilder

May your love be perfect, even if you are not. ❤
—Michael Macfarlane

Love never ends; . . . So faith, hope, love abide, these three; but the greatest of these is love. ❤
—I Corinthians 13:4-8, 13

Love is patient and kind; love is not jealous or boastful; it is not arrogant or rude. Love does not insist on its own way; it is not irritable or resentful; it does not rejoice at wrong, but rejoices in the right. Love bears all things, believes all things, hopes all things, endures all things. ❤

To love someone is to see a miracle invisible to others. ❤ —Francois Mauriac

Don't hold so tight that you squeeze one another away. ❤

The sum which two married people owe to one another defies calculation. It is an infinite debt, which can only be discharged through all eternity. ❤ —Goethe

It is the man and woman united that makes the complete human being. Separate she lacks his force of body and strength of reason; he her softness, sensibility and acute discernment. Together they are most likely to succeed in the world. ❤ —Benjamin Franklin

Toasts to Just the Groom

To keep your marriage brimming;
With love in the loving cup,
Whenever you're wrong, admit it;
Whenever you're right; shut up! ❤ —Ogden Nash

To your good health, old friend,
may you live for a thousand years,
and I be there to count them. ♥
—Robert Smith Surtees

As a man thinketh in his heart, so is he. ♥
—Proverbs 23:7

The most precious possession that ever comes to a man
in this world is a woman's heart. ♥
—Josiah Gilbert Holland

My wish for you is that you will marry someone so
great that it will take an entire lifetime to know every-
thing about her. ♥ —Charlie W. Shedd

Today's the day, Tonight's the night,
We've shot the stork—So you're all right! ♥

Here's to the present—and to hell with the past!
A health to the future and joy to the last! ♥

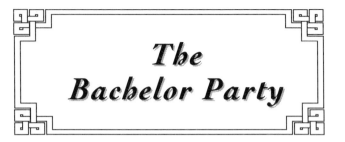

The Bachelor Party

*A*lthough the bachelor party was traditionally held the night before the wedding, it is becoming much more accepted to have it the weekend before. This gives plenty of time to recuperate and allows for the wedding rehearsal to be the night before the wedding.

This party is usually hosted by the best man, but it is not uncommon today for you to be a co-host with one or more of the groom's male relatives, family members, or close friends.

Generally, you invite all male members of the wedding party, along with other close friends and family. The fathers of the groom and bride may be included on the invitation list, but if they do attend, they will probably stay for only a short time.

The traditional purpose of the bachelor party was for the groom-to-be to celebrate his last night out on the town as a bachelor. Bachelor parties of today which seek to follow tradition often include visits to burlesque shows or casinos, or are held in hotel rooms with strippers and high-stakes poker games.

Some bachelor parties, however, are more contemporary in scope and are intended to provide close camaraderie with attendance to a rousing softball game followed by dinner. Or the party might consist of a quiet poker game with catered deli sandwiches for the event.

The style and atmosphere of the party will depend a great deal on the personality of you and the groom. Regardless of whether it is a sedate gathering that includes dinner and quiet entertainment or a wild celebration, it should be an event where only men are invited and only men attend. No wives, or girlfriends should show up unexpectedly, unless the giver of the party decides to break tradition and invites them to attend.

The bachelor party may be the time you choose to give the groom the gift from yourself and the ushers. If, however, the evening's activities are planned to be on the wild side, the gift may be lost or broken and certainly not fully appreciated. Under these circumstances, you will want to synchronize your gift giving with the groom and choose the rehearsal dinner as a better time.

The gift you select to give to the groom should be personal and lasting in nature. It could be an engraved money clip, a hand-tooled leather wallet, a monogrammed bathrobe, engraved wine goblets, or a fashionable pen.

The bachelor party can be hosted at your home, a friend's house, or a popular restaurant or bar. To follow a time-honored tradition, everyone, led by the groom or by you, toasts the bride, with some going as far as to break the glass so that it may never be used for a less worthy cause.

(The host of the party is responsible for paying for the broken glasses and should notify the management ahead of time, so that they know exactly what to expect and do not serve their finest crystal for the event.)

You, as the best man, should consult with the groom and his new bride about your plans for the bachelor party. Or, if the bride-to-be mentions her concerns, you should make certain she feels free to talk openly with you and the groom about any and all concerns she may have about the party activities that you may have planned.

You, as the host, must make certain that if drinking of alcoholic beverages will be part of the bachelor party, that arrangements have been made for safe rides home or for designated drivers.

Today many couples whose friends are single are combining the bachelor and bachelorette party into one celebration. It is a perfect time for attendants, groomsmen and other friends to form new friendships of their own.

Best Man's Checklist

The following are comprehensive, user-friendly checklists to help you, the best man, keep track of your responsibilities. Consult with the bride and groom as you fill them out, and then give each a copy.

However, if you're just not able to perform all of the duties outlined below, just remember, skipping the ceremony is not an option!

Best Man (This is you, in case you forget!)

Name   _____

Phone   _____

Address   _____

_____

_____

Best Man (continued)

Travel Arrangements—

Airline _____

Arrival Date _____

Arrival Time _____

Transportation from Airport _____

_____

Departure Date _____

Departure Time _____

Accommodations—

_____

_____

_____

Special Duties—

_____

_____

_____

_____

_____

Ushers/Groomsmen
Head Usher _____
Phone _____
Address _____

_____

Travel Arrangements—
Airline _____
Arrival Date _____
Arrival Time _____
Transportation from Airport _____

_____

Departure Date _____
Departure Time _____

Accommodations _____

_____

Special Duties _____

_____

_____

Ushers/Groomsmen (continued)
Usher _____
Phone _____
Address _____

_____

Travel Arrangements—
Airline _____
Arrival Date _____
Arrival Time _____
Transportation from Airport _____

_____

Departure Date _____
Departure Time _____

Accommodations _____

_____

Special Duties _____

_____

_____

_____

Usher _____

Phone _____

Address _____

_____

Travel Arrangements—

Airline _____

Arrival Date _____

Arrival Time _____

Transportation from Airport _____

_____

Departure Date _____

Departure Time _____

Accommodations _____

_____

Special Duties _____

_____

_____

_____

_____

Ushers/Groomsmen (continued)

Usher _____

Phone _____

Address _____

_____

Travel Arrangements—

Airline _____

Arrival Date _____

Arrival Time _____

Transportation from Airport _____

_____

Departure Date _____

Departure Time _____

Accommodations _____

_____

Special Duties _____

_____

_____

_____

Usher _____

Phone _____

Address _____

_____

Travel Arrangements—

Airline _____

Arrival Date _____

Arrival Time _____

Transportation from Airport _____

_____

Departure Date _____

Departure Time _____

Accommodations _____

_____

Special Duties _____

_____

_____

_____

_____

Ushers/Groomsmen (continued)

Usher _____

Phone _____

Address _____

_____

Travel Arrangements—

Airline _____

Arrival Date _____

Arrival Time _____

Transportation from Airport _____

_____

Departure Date _____

Departure Time _____

Accommodations _____

_____

Special Duties _____

_____

_____

_____

Usher _____

Phone _____

Address _____

_____

Travel Arrangements—

Airline _____

Arrival Date _____

Arrival Time _____

Transportation from Airport _____

_____

Departure Date _____

Departure Time _____

Accommodations _____

_____

Special Duties _____

_____

_____

_____

_____

Ushers/Groomsmen (continued)
Usher _____

Phone _____

Address _____

_____

Travel Arrangements—

Airline _____

Arrival Date _____

Arrival Time _____

Transportation from Airport _____

_____

Departure Date _____

Departure Time _____

Accommodations _____

_____

Special Duties _____

_____

_____

_____

Ring Bearer
Name _____

Parent's Name_____

Phone _____

Address _____

_____

Travel Arrangements—

Airline _____

Arrival Date _____

Arrival Time _____

Transportation from Airport _____

_____

Departure Date _____

Departure Time _____

Accommodations _____

_____

Special Duties _____

_____

Special Duties of the Best Man—

Parties to attend:

Party #1 _____

Date _____

Time _____

Place _____

Gift _____

Notes _____

_____

_____

_____

Party #2 _____

Date _____

Time _____

Place _____

Gift _____

Notes _____

_____

_____

_____

_____

Party #3 _____

Date _____

Time _____

Place _____

Gift _____

Notes _____

_____

_____

_____

_____

Party #4 _____

Date _____

Time _____

Place _____

Gift _____

Notes _____

_____

_____

_____

_____

_____

Rehearsal

Date _____
Time _____
Place _____
Attire _____
Notes _____

_____
_____
_____
_____
_____

Rehearsal Dinner

Date _____
Time _____
Place _____
Attire _____
Notes _____

_____
_____
_____
_____

Bachelor Party

Host/s _____

Phone _____

Date _____

Time _____

Place _____

Attire _____

Activities _____

_____

_____

_____

_____

Menu _____

_____

_____

Cost per Plate _____

Total Cost _____

Bartender _____

Phone _____

Arrival Time _____

Departure Time _____

Bachelor Party (continued)

Bar Beverages _____

_____

Cost _____

Invitations _____

_____

_____

Guest List—
Name _____
Phone _____
Address _____

_____

Name _____
Phone _____
Address _____

_____

Name _____
Phone _____
Address _____

_____

Name _____
Phone _____
Address _____

Name _____
Phone _____
Address _____

Name _____
Phone _____
Address _____

Name _____
Phone _____
Address _____

Name _____
Phone _____
Address _____

Bachelor Party (continued)

Name _____

Phone _____

Address _____

_____

Name _____

Phone _____

Address _____

_____

Name _____

Phone _____

Address _____

_____

Name _____

Phone _____

Address _____

_____

Name _____

Phone _____

Address _____

_____

Arranged Transportation Home—

_____
_____
_____
_____

Total Cost _____
Notes   _____
_____
_____
_____
_____

Groom's Gift
Gift _____
Store _____
Address _____
_____
Phone _____
Gift Cost _____

Groom's Gift (continued)

Engraving Cost _____

Order Date _____

Pick-up Date _____

Words to Be Engraved _____

_____

_____

Money Collected from Groomsmen—

Name _____

Amount _____

Name _____

Amount _____

Name _____

Amount _____

Name _____

Amount _____

Name _____

Amount _____

Name _____

Amount _____

Total Amount Collected _____

Total Cost of Gift _____

Date to Present to Groom _____

Bridal Couple Gift

Gift _____

Store _____

Address _____

_____

Phone _____

Order Date _____

Pick-up Date _____

Cost _____

Presentation Date to Couple _____

Duties Before the Ceremony

1. Arrange for Flowers or Champagne to Be Delivered to Honeymoon Suite.

   Hotel _____

   Date _____

   Item _____

   Card _____

2. Arrange to Help Groom Pack.

   Date _____

   Time _____

   Place _____

   Items—

   _____

   _____

   _____

   _____

   _____

   _____

   _____

3. Meet with Groom to Arrange Transportation.
   Date _____
   Time _____
   Place _____
   Transportation to Ceremony _____
   _____
   Driver _____
   Transportation to Reception _____
   _____
   Driver _____

   Transportation Following Reception —
   _____
   _____
   Location _____
   Time _____

4. Pick up Groom's Formal Wear.
   Date _____
   Place _____
   Address _____

Duties Before Ceremony (continued)

Time _____

Items to Be Picked Up _____

_____

_____

_____

_____

_____

To Be Delivered _____

Date _____

Time _____

Place _____

5. Payment Checks for Wedding Participants.
   Wedding Officiant _____
   Others _____

   _____

   _____

   _____

   _____

   _____

6. Locate and Place Marriage License So that It Can Be Signed After the Ceremony.

_____

_____

Reserved Section Seating Chart

First Pew — Bride's Section _____

_____

_____

_____

First Pew — Groom's Section _____

_____

_____

_____

Second Pew — Bride's Section _____

_____

_____

_____

Second Pew — Groom's Section _____

_____

_____

_____

Reserved Section Seating Chart (continued)

Third Pew — Bride's Section _____

_____

_____

_____

Third Pew — Groom's Section _____

_____

_____

_____

Names of Other Special Relatives or Friends

_____

_____

_____

Duties During the Ceremony

_____

_____

_____

_____

_____

_____

Duties After the Ceremony/Before the Reception

_____
_____
_____
_____
_____
_____
_____

Duties During the Reception

Family Members to Be Introduced —
Bride's Parents   _____

_____

Groom's Parents _____

_____

Bride's Immediate Family   _____

_____
_____
_____
_____

Duties During the Reception (continued)

Groom's Immediate Family _____

_____

_____

_____

_____

Wedding Officiant_____

Out-of-Town Relatives _____

_____

_____

_____

Out-of-Town Guests _____

_____

_____

_____

_____

_____

Important Friends   _____

_____

_____

_____

Toast _____

_____

_____

_____

_____

_____

_____

_____

_____

_____

_____

Duties After the Reception
Transportation for Bride/Groom —

_____

_____

_____

Location of Transportation _____

_____

_____

Duties After the Reception

Deliver Gifts —
Address _____

_____

Phone _____
Date _____

Deposit Wedding Money/Checks—
Bank _____
Address _____

_____

Checks Deposited—
Giver _____

_____

Amount _____

Giver _____

_____

Amount _____

Giver _____

Amount _____

Giver _____

Amount _____

Giver _____

Amount _____

Giver _____

Amount _____

Cash Deposited—
Giver _____

Amount _____

Duties After the Reception (continued)

Giver _____

_____

Amount _____

Giver _____

_____

Amount _____

Giver _____

_____

Amount _____

Giver _____

_____

Amount _____

Return Groomsmen's Formal Wear —
Address _____

_____

Phone _____

Date _____

Time _____

Groomsmen Attire Included for Return —

_____

_____

_____

Important Names of Wedding Party

Bride's Parents _____

_____

_____

Address _____

_____

_____

_____

Phone _____ _

Groom's Parents _____

_____

_____

Important Names of Wedding Party (continued)

Address _____

_____

Phone _____

Maid/Matron-of-Honor _____

_____

Address _____

_____

Phone _____

Wedding Coordinator _____

_____

Address _____

_____

Phone _____

Wedding Officiant _____

_____

Address _____

_____

Phone _____

Time of Arrival _____

Ceremony Site _____

Person in Charge_____

Address _____

_____

Phone _____

Reception Site _____

Person in Charge_____

Address _____

_____

Phone _____

Caterer _____

Person in Charge_____

Address _____

_____

Phone _____

Time of Arrival _____

Time of Departure _____

Important Names of Wedding Party (continued)

Bartender _____

Address _____

_____

Phone _____

Time of Arrival _____

Time of Departure _____

Photographer _____

Address _____

_____

Phone _____

Time of Arrival _____

Times to Take Planned Pictures —

Time 1 _____

Persons Included _____

_____

_____

_____

_____

Time 2_____

Persons Included_____

_____

_____

_____

_____

Time 3_____

Persons Included_____

_____

_____

_____

_____

_____

_____

_____

Florist _____

Address_____

_____

Phone _____

Arrival Time _____

Important Names of Wedding Party (continued)

Musicians _____

Person in Charge _____

Address _____

_____

Phone _____

Time of Arrival _____

Time of Departure _____

Special Announcements

_____

_____

_____

_____

_____

_____

_____

_____

_____

_____

_____

Special Requests

_____
_____
_____
_____
_____
_____
_____
_____
_____
_____
_____
_____
_____
_____
_____
_____
_____
_____
_____
_____

Index